The Longman Anthology of World Literature

━━━◆◆◆━━━

VOLUME C

THE EARLY MODERN PERIOD

David Damrosch
COLUMBIA UNIVERSITY
The Ancient Near East; Mesoamerica

April Alliston
PRINCETON UNIVERSITY
The Age of the Enlightenment

Marshall Brown
UNIVERSITY OF WASHINGTON
The Nineteenth Century

Page duBois
UNIVERSITY OF CALIFORNIA, SAN DIEGO
Classical Greece

Sabry Hafez
UNIVERSITY OF LONDON
Arabic and Islamic Literatures

Ursula K. Heise
COLUMBIA UNIVERSITY
The Twentieth Century

Djelal Kadir
PENNSYLVANIA STATE UNIVERSITY
The Twentieth Century

David L. Pike
AMERICAN UNIVERSITY
Rome and the Roman Empire; Medieval Europe

Sheldon Pollock
UNIVERSITY OF CHICAGO
South Asia

Bruce Robbins
COLUMBIA UNIVERSITY
The Nineteenth Century

Haruo Shirane
COLUMBIA UNIVERSITY
Japan

Jane Tylus
NEW YORK UNIVERSITY
Early Modern Europe

Pauline Yu
AMERICAN COUNCIL OF LEARNED SOCIETIES
China

The Longman Anthology of World Literature

David Damrosch

General Editor

VOLUME C

THE EARLY MODERN PERIOD

Jane Tylus

David Damrosch

with contributions by

Pauline Yu and Sheldon Pollock

PEARSON
Longman

New York   San Francisco   Boston
London   Toronto   Sydney   Tokyo   Singapore   Madrid
Mexico City   Munich   Paris   Cape Town   Hong Kong   Montreal

Vice President and Editor-in-Chief: *Joseph Terry*
Development Manager: *Janet Lanphier*
Development Editor: *Adam Beroud*
Senior Marketing Manager: *Melanie Craig*
Senior Supplements Editor: *Donna Campion*
Media Supplements Editor: *Nancy Garcia*
Production Manager: *Douglas Bell*
Project Coordination, Text Design, and Page Makeup: *Elm Street Publishing Services, Inc.*
Senior Design Manager/Cover Designer: *Nancy Danahy*
On the Cover: Detail from *The Geographer,* oil on canvas, by Johannes Vermeer
  (1632–1675). Copyright © The Granger Collection.
Photo Research: *Photosearch, Inc.*
Manufacturing Buyer: *Lucy Hebard*
Printer and Binder: *Quebecor-World/Taunton*
Cover Printer: *The Lehigh Press, Inc.*

For permission to use copyrighted material, grateful acknowledgment is made to the copyright
holders on pages 895–898, which are hereby made part of this copyright page.

Library of Congress Cataloging-in-Publication Data

The Longman anthology of world literature / David Damrosch, general editor.—1st ed.
    v.   cm.
  Includes bibliographical references and index.
  Contents: v. A. The ancient world—v. B. The medieval era—v. C. The early
modern period—v. D. The seventeenth and eighteenth centuries—v. E. The
nineteenth century—v. F. The twentieth century.
  ISBN 0-321-05533-0 (v. A).—ISBN 0-321-16978-6 (v. B).— 0-321-16979-4
  (v. C).— 0-321-16980-8 (v. D).— 0-321-17306-6 (v. E).— 0-321-05536-5 (v. F).
  1. Literature—Collections.   2. Literature—History and criticism.
I. Damrosch, David.
PN6013.L66   2004
808.8—dc22
                                                                2003061890

Please visit us at http://www.ablongman.com/damrosch.

To place your order, please use the following ISBN numbers:

ISBN Volume One Package *The Ancient World to The Early Modern Period*
(includes Volumes A, B, and C): **0-321-20238-4**

ISBN Volume Two Package *The Seventeenth Century to The Twentieth Century*
(includes Volumes D, E, and F): **0-321-20237-6**

Or, to order individual volumes, please use the following ISBN numbers:

ISBN Volume A, *The Ancient World:* 0-321-05533-0
ISBN Volume B, *The Medieval Era:* 0-321-16978-6
ISBN Volume C, *The Early Modern Period:* 0-321-16979-4
ISBN Volume D, *The Seventeenth and Eighteenth Centuries:* 0-321-16980-8
ISBN Volume E, *The Nineteenth Century:* 0-321-17306-6
ISBN Volume F, *The Twentieth Century:* 0-321-05536-5

1 2 3 4 5 6 7 8 9 10—QWT—06 05 04 03

CONTENTS

Early Modern Europe   149

⇌✦ PERSPECTIVES ✦⇌
Lyric Sequences and Self-Definition   226

FRANÇOIS RABELAIS (c. 1494–1553)   332

Mesoamerica:
Before Columbus and After Cortés   761

⇒✦ PERSPECTIVES ✦⇐
The Conquest and Its Aftermath   810

LIST OF ILLUSTRATIONS

Color Plates *following page 6*

Black-and-White Images

Maps

On the Cover

Detail from Johannes Vermeer, *The Geographer,* 1669. Holding a divider for measuring distances, a geographer looks up from his books and charts to plot the course of exploration in his mind's eye. Vermeer loved to paint intimate domestic spaces, into which the wider world subtly intrudes in the form of a visitor, or a letter, or a painting. Here, maps surround the geographer; a large vellum sea chart is rolled up beside him, more maps are scattered around the floor, and hanging on the wall (see the full image on the back cover) is a map of "all the seacoasts of Europe." The globe on the chest was made in 1618 by the Dutch geographer Jodocus Hondius (whose own portrait can be seen in the world map by his son Hendricus, on the inside front cover of this volume); Vermeer has positioned the globe to show the Indian Ocean. "The geographer" is probably the Dutch scientist Anton van Leeuwenhoek, who passed his examination as a surveyor in February of 1669, the year this painting was made. He shared Vermeer's fascination with optics and was a pioneer in the development of the microscope; he became the executor of Vermeer's estate after his death in 1675. This painting and a companion piece, *The Astronomer,* dramatize the excitement of the new sciences of exploration and discovery being developed during the early modern period.

PREFACE

Our world today is both expanding and growing smaller at the same time. Expanding, through a tremendous increase in the range of cultures that actively engage with each other; and yet growing smaller as well, as people and products surge across borders in the process known as globalization. This double movement creates remarkable opportunities for cross-cultural understanding, as well as new kinds of tensions, miscommunications, and uncertainties. Both the opportunities and the uncertainties are amply illustrated in the changing shape of world literature. A generation ago, when the term "world literature" was used in North America, it largely meant masterworks by European writers from Homer onward, together with a few favored North American writers, heirs to the Europeans. Today, however, it is generally recognized that Europe is only part of the story of the world's literatures, and only part of the story of North America's cultural heritage. An extraordinary range of exciting material is now in view, from the earliest Sumerian lyrics inscribed on clay tablets to the latest Kashmiri poetry circulated on the Internet. Many new worlds—and newly visible *older* worlds of classical traditions around the globe—await us today.

How can we best approach such varied materials from so many cultures? Can we deal with this embarrassment of riches without being overwhelmed by it, and without merely giving a glancing regard to less familiar traditions? This anthology has been designed to help readers successfully navigate "the sea of stories"—as Salman Rushdie has described the world's literary heritage. This preface will outline the ways we've gone about this challenging, fascinating task.

CONNECTING DISTINCTIVE TRADITIONS

Works of world literature engage in a double conversation: with their culture of origin and with the varied contexts into which they travel away from home. To look broadly at world literature is therefore to see patterns of difference as well as points of contact and commonality. The world's disparate traditions have developed very distinct kinds of literature, even very different ideas as to what should be called "literature" at all. This anthology uses a variety of means to showcase what is most distinctive and also what is commonly shared among the world's literatures. Throughout the anthology, we employ three kinds of grouping:

☞ CROSSCURRENTS: A major grouping at the beginning of each volume, bringing together literary responses to worldwide developments.

☞ PERSPECTIVES: Groupings that provide cultural context for major works, illuminating issues of broad importance.

☞ RESONANCES: Sources for a specific text or responses to it, often from a different time and place.

The "Crosscurrents" sections that open our six volumes highlight overarching issues or developments that many cultures have faced, often in conversation with neighboring cultures and more distant ones too. "Creation Myths and Social Realities" in antiquity, for example, brings together creation stories that circulated throughout the ancient Near East, westward to Greece, and eastward to India. "The Folk and Their Tales" in the nineteenth century shows the interplay of folk traditions between India and Europe, Africa and the Americas, Native Americans and Euro-Americans.

Regional divisions predominate in our Volumes A through C, reflecting the distinctive development of the world's major literary traditions over the centuries before the modern period. For each of these volumes, the Crosscurrents provide an initial, cross-cutting overview of a major issue, giving a reminder that there have been important contacts across cultures as far back as we know—and showing too how different cultures can independently address matters of common human concern. In our more globally organized later volumes D through F (mid-seventeenth century to the present), the Crosscurrents demonstrate the increasing interconnectedness of the world's literary traditions.

Throughout the anthology, our many "Perspectives" sections provide cultural context for the major works around them, giving insight into such issues as the representation of death and immortality (in the ancient Near East); the meeting of Christians, Muslims, and Jews in medieval Iberia; the idea of the national poet in the nineteenth century; and "modernist memory" in the twentieth. Perspectives sections also provide an opportunity for focused regional groupings within our globally structured later volumes, with "Other Americas" in the nineteenth century, for example, and "Modernism and Revolution in Russia" in the twentieth. Perspectives sections give a range of voices and views, strategies and styles, in highly readable textual groupings. The Perspectives groupings serve a major pedagogical as well as intellectual purpose in making these selections accessible and useful within the time constraints of a survey course.

Finally, our "Resonances" perform the crucial function of linking works across time as well as space. For Homer's *Iliad,* a Resonance shows oral composition as it is still practiced today north of Greece, while for the *Odyssey* we have Resonances giving modern responses to Homer by Franz Kafka, Derek Walcott, and the Greek poet George Seferis. Accompanying the traditional Navajo "Story of the Emergence" (Volume E) is an extended selection from *Black Elk Speaks* which shows how ancient imagery infused the dream visions of the Sioux healer and warrior Nicholas Black Elk, helping him deal with the crises of lost land and independence that his people were facing. Resonances for Conrad's *Heart of Darkness* (Volume F) give selections from Conrad's diary of his own journey upriver in the Congo, and a speech by Henry Morton Stanley, the explorer-journalist who was serving as publicist for King Leopold's exploitation of his colony in the years just before Conrad went there. Stanley's surreal speech—in which he calculates how much money the Manchester weavers can make providing wedding dresses and burial clothes for the Congolese— gives a vivid instance of the outlook, and the rhetoric, that Conrad grimly parodies in Mr. Kurtz and his associates.

PRINCIPLES OF SELECTION

Beyond our immediate groupings, our overall selections have been made with an eye to fostering connections across time and space: a Perspectives section on "Courtly Women" in medieval Japan (Volume B) introduces themes that can be followed up in

"Court Culture and Female Authorship" in Enlightenment-era Europe (Volume D), while the ancient Mediterranean and South Asian creation myths at the start of Volume A find echoes in later cosmic-creation narratives from Iceland (Volume B), Mesoamerica (Volume C), and indigenous peoples today (Volume E). Altogether, we have worked to create an exceptionally coherent and well-integrated presentation of an extraordinary variety of works from around the globe, from the dawn of writing to the present.

Recognizing that different sorts of works have counted as literature in differing times and places, we take an inclusive approach, centering on poems, plays, and fictional narratives but also including selections from rich historical, religious, and philosophical texts like Plato's *Republic* and the Qur'an that have been important for much later literary work, even though they weren't conceived as literature themselves. We present many complete masterworks, including *The Epic of Gilgamesh* (in a beautiful verse translation), Homer's *Odyssey,* Dante's *Inferno,* and Chinua Achebe's *Things Fall Apart,* and we have extensive, teachable selections from such long works as *The Tale of Genji, Don Quixote,* and both parts of Goethe's *Faust.*

Along with these major selections we present a great array of shorter works, some of which have been known only to specialists and only now are entering into world literature. It is our experience as readers and as teachers that the established classics themselves can best be understood when they're set in a varied literary landscape. Nothing is included here, though, simply to make a point: whether world-renowned or recently rediscovered, these are compelling works to read. Throughout our work on this book, we've tried to be highly inclusive in principle and yet carefully selective in practice, avoiding tokenism and also its inverse, the piling up of an unmanageable array of heterogeneous material. If we've succeeded as we hope, the result will be coherent as well as capacious, substantive as well as stimulating.

LITERATURE, ART, AND MUSIC

One important way to understand literary works in context is to read them in conjunction with the broader social and artistic culture in which they were created. Literature has often had a particularly close relation to visual art and to music. Different as the arts are in their specific resources and techniques, a culture's artistic expressions often share certain family resemblances, common traits that can be seen across different media—and that may even come out more clearly in visual or musical form than in translations of literature itself. This anthology includes dozens of black-and-white illustrations and a suite of color illustrations in each volume, chosen to work in close conjunction with our literary selections. Some of these images directly illustrate literary works, while others show important aspects of a culture's aesthetic sensibility. Often, writing actually appears on paintings and sculptures, with represented people and places sharing the space with beautifully rendered Mayan hieroglyphs, Arabic calligraphy, or Chinese brushstrokes.

Music too has been a close companion of literary creation and performance. Our very term "lyric" refers to the lyres or harps with which the Greeks accompanied poems as they were sung. In China, the first major literary work is the *Book of Songs.* In Europe too, until quite recent times poetry was often sung and even prose was usually read aloud. We have created two audio CDs to accompany the anthology, one for Volumes A through C and one for Volumes D through F. These CDs give a wealth of poetry and music from the cultures we feature in the anthology; they are both a valuable teaching resource and also a pure pleasure to listen to.

AIDS TO UNDERSTANDING

A major emphasis of our work has been to introduce each culture and each work to best effect. Each major period and section of the anthology, each grouping of works, and each individual author has an introduction by a member of our editorial team. Our goal has been to write introductions informed by deep knowledge worn lightly. Neither talking down to our readers nor overwhelming them with masses of unassimilable information, our introductions don't seek to "cover" the material but instead try to uncover it, to provide ways in and connections outward. Similarly, our footnotes and glosses are concise and informative, rather than massive or interpretive. Time lines for each volume, and maps and pronunciation guides throughout the anthology, all aim to foster an informed and pleasurable reading of the works.

GOING FURTHER

The Longman Anthology of World Literature makes connections beyond its covers as well as within them. Bibliographies at the end of each volume point the way to historical and critical readings for students wishing to go into greater depth for term papers. The Companion Website we've developed for the course (www.ablongman.com/worldlit) gives a wealth of links to excellent Web resources on all our major texts and many related historical and cultural movements and events. The Web site includes an audio version of our printed pronunciation guides: you can simply click on a name to hear it pronounced. Finally, the Web site includes readings of works in the original and in translation, with accompanying texts, giving extensive exposure to the aural dimension of many of the languages represented in the anthology.

For instructors, we have also created an extensive, two-volume instructor's manual, *Teaching World Literature*—written directly by the editors themselves, drawing on our years of experience in teaching these materials.

TRANSLATION ACROSS CULTURES

The circulation of world literature is always an exercise in cultural translation, and one way to define works of world literature is that they are the works that gain in translation. Some great texts remain so intimately tied to their point of origin that they never read well abroad; they may have an abiding importance at home, but don't play a role in the wider world. Other works, though, gain in resonance as they move out into new contexts, new conjunctions. Edgar Allan Poe found his first really serious readers in France, rather than in the United States. *The Thousand and One Nights,* long a marginal work in Arabic traditions oriented toward poetry rather than popular prose, gained new readers and new influence abroad, and Scheherazade's intricately nested tales now help us in turn to read the European tales of Boccaccio and Marguerite de Navarre with new attention and appreciation. A Perspectives section on *"The Thousand and One Nights* in the Twentieth Century" (Volume F) brings together a range of Arab, European, and American writers who have continued to plumb its riches to this day.

As important as cultural translation in general is the issue of actual translation from one language to another. We have sought out compelling translations for all our foreign-language works, and periodically we offer our readers the opportunity to think directly about the issue of translation. Sometimes we offer distinctively different translations of differing works from a single author or source: for the Bible, for example, we give Genesis 1–11 in Robert Alter's lively, oral-style translation, while we give selected psalms in the magnificent King James Version and the Joseph story in the lucid New International Version. Our selections from Homer's *Iliad* appear in Richmond Lattimore's stately older translation, while Homer's *Odyssey* is given in Robert Fagles's eloquent new version.

At other times, we give alternative translations of a single work. So we have Chinese lyrics translated by the modernist poet Ezra Pound and by a contemporary scholar; and we have Petrarch sonnets translated by the Renaissance English poet Thomas Wyatt and also by contemporary translators. These juxtapositions can show some of the varied ways in which translators over the centuries have sought to carry works over from one time and place to another—not so much by mirroring and reflecting an unchanged meaning, as by refracting it, in a prismatic process that can add new highlights and reveal new facets in a classic text. At times, when we haven't found a translation that really satisfies us, we've translated the work ourselves—an activity we recommend to all who wish to come to know a work from the inside.

We hope that the results of our years of work on this project will be as enjoyable to use as the book has been to create. We welcome you now inside our pages.

David Damrosch

ACKNOWLEDGMENTS

In the extended process of planning and preparing this anthology, the editors have been fortunate to have the support, advice, and assistance of many people. Our editor, Joe Terry, and our publisher, Roth Wilkofsky, have supported our project in every possible way and some seemingly impossible ones as well, helping us produce the best possible book despite all challenges to budgets and well-laid plans in a rapidly evolving field. Their associates Janet Lanphier and Melanie Craig have shown unwavering enthusiasm and constant creativity in developing the book and its related Web site and audio CDs and in introducing the results to the world. Our development editors, first Mark Getlein and then Adam Beroud, have shown a compelling blend of literary acuity and quiet diplomacy in guiding thirteen far-flung editors through the many stages of work. Peter Meyers brought great energy and creativity to work on our CDs. Donna Campion and Dianne Hall worked diligently to complete the instructor's manual. Celeste Parker-Bates cleared hundreds and hundreds of text permissions from publishers in many countries, and Sherri Zuckerman at Photosearch, Inc., cleared our many photo permissions.

Once the manuscript was complete, Doug Bell, the production manager, oversaw the simultaneous production of six massive books on a tight and shifting schedule. Valerie Zaborski, managing editor in production, also helped and, along the way, developed a taste for the good-humored fatalism of Icelandic literature. Our lead copyeditor, Stephanie Magean, and her associates Martha Beyerlein, Elizabeth Jahaske, and Marcia LaBrenz marvelously integrated everyone's writing, and then Amber Allen and her colleagues at Elm Street Publishing Services worked overtime to produce beautiful books accurate down to the last exotic accent.

We are specifically grateful for the guidance of the many reviewers who advised us on the creation of this book: Roberta Adams (Fitchburg State College); Adetutu Abatan (Floyd College); Magda al-Nowaihi (Columbia University); Nancy Applegate (Floyd College); Susan Atefat-Peckham (Georgia College and State University); Evan Balkan (CCBC-Catonsville); Michelle Barnett (University of Alabama, Birmingham); Colonel Bedell (Virginia Military Institute); Thomas Beebee (Pennsylvania State University); Paula Berggren (Baruch College); Mark Bernier (Blinn College); Ronald Bogue (University of Georgia); Terre Burton (Dixie State College); Patricia Cearley (South Plains College); Raj Chekuri (Laredo Community College); Sandra Clark (University of Wyoming); Thomas F. Connolly (Suffolk University); Vilashini Cooppan (Yale University); Bradford Crain (College of the Ozarks); Robert W. Croft (Gainesville College); Frank Day (Clemson University); Michael Delahoyde (Washington State University); Elizabeth Otten Delmonico (Truman State University); Jo Devine (University of Alaska Southeast); Gene Doty (University of Missouri—Rolla); James Earle (University of Oregon); R. Steve Eberly (Western Carolina University); Walter Evans (Augusta State University); Fidel Fajardo-Acosta (Creighton University); Mike Felker (South Plains College); Janice Gable (Valley Forge Christian College); Stanley Galloway (Bridgewater College); Doris Gardenshire (Trinity Valley Community College); Jonathan Glenn (University of Central Arkansas); Dean Hall (Kansas State University); Dorothy Hardman (Fort Valley State

University); Elissa Heil (University of the Ozarks); David Hesla (Emory University); Susan Hillabold (Purdue University North Central); Karen Hodges (Texas Wesleyan); David Hoegberg (Indiana University-Purdue University—Indianapolis); Sheri Hoem (Xavier University); Michael Hutcheson (Landmark College); Mary Anne Hutchinson (Utica College); Raymond Ide (Lancaster Bible College); James Ivory (Appalachian State University); Craig Kallendorf (Texas A & M University); Bridget Keegan (Creighton University); Steven Kellman (University of Texas—San Antonio); Roxanne Kent-Drury (Northern Kentucky University); Susan Kroeg (Eastern Kentucky University); Tamara Kuzmenkov (Tacoma Community College); Robert Lorenzi (Camden County College—Blackwood); Mark Mazzone (Tennessee State University); David McCracken (Coker College); George Mitrenski (Auburn University); James Nicholl (Western Carolina University); Roger Osterholm (Embry-Riddle University); Joe Pellegrino (Eastern Kentucky University); Linda Lang-Peralta (Metropolitan State College of Denver); Sandra Petree (University of Arkansas); David E. Phillips (Charleston Southern University); Terry Reilly (University of Alaska); Constance Relihan (Auburn University); Nelljean Rice (Coastal Carolina University); Colleen Richmond (George Fox University); Gretchen Ronnow (Wayne State University); John Rothfork (West Texas A & M University); Elise Salem-Manganaro (Fairleigh Dickinson University); Asha Sen (University of Wisconsin Eau Claire); Richard Sha (American University); Edward Shaw (University of Central Florida); Jack Shreve (Allegany College of Maryland); Jimmy Dean Smith (Union College); Floyd C. Stuart (Norwich University); Eleanor Sumpter-Latham (Central Oregon Community College); Ron Swigger (Albuquerque Technical Vocational Institute); Barry Tharaud (Mesa State College); Theresa Thompson (Valdosta State College); Teresa Thonney (Columbia Basin College); Charles Tita (Shaw University); Scott D. Vander Ploeg (Madisonville Community College); Marian Wernicke (Pensacola Junior College); Sallie Wolf (Arapahoe Community College); and Dede Yow (Kennesaw State University).

We also wish to express our gratitude to the reviewers who gave us additional advice on the book's companion Web site: Nancy Applegate (Floyd College); James Earl (University of Oregon); David McCracken (Coker College); Linda Lang-Peralta (Metropolitan State College of Denver); Asha Sen (University of Wisconsin—Eau Claire); Jimmy Dean Smith (Union College); Floyd Stuart (Norwich University); and Marian Wernicke (Pensacola Junior College).

The editors were assisted in tracking down texts and information by wonderfully able research assistants: Kerry Bystrom, Julie Lapiski, Katalin Lovasz, Joseph Ortiz, Laura B. Sayre, and Lauren Simonetti. April Alliston wishes to thank Brandon Lafving for his invaluable comments on her drafts and Gregory Maertz for his knowledge and support. Marshall Brown would like to thank his research assistant Françoise Belot for her help and Jane K. Brown for writing the Goethe introduction. Sheldon Pollock would like to thank Whitney Cox, Rajeev Kinra, Susanne Mrozik, and Guriqbal Sahota for their assistance and Haruo Shirane thanks Michael Brownstein for writing the introduction to Hozumi Ikan, and Akiko Takeuchi for writing the introductions to the Noh drama.

It has been a great pleasure to work with all these colleagues both at Longman and at schools around the country. This book exists for its readers, whose reactions and suggestions we warmly welcome, as *The Longman Anthology of World Literature* moves out into the world.

ABOUT THE EDITORS

David Damrosch (Columbia University). His books include *The Narrative Covenant: Transformations of Genre in the Growth of Biblical Literature* (1987), *Meetings of the Mind* (2000), and *What Is World Literature?* (2003). He has been president of the American Comparative Literature Association (2001–2003) and is general editor of *The Longman Anthology of British Literature* (1998; second edition, 2002).

April Alliston (Princeton University). Author of *Virtue's Faults: Correspondence in Eighteenth-Century British and French Women's Fiction* (1996), and editor of Sophia Lee's *The Recess* (2000). Her book on concepts of character, gender, and plausibility in Enlightenment historical narratives is forthcoming.

Marshall Brown (University of Washington). Author of *The Shape of German Romanticism* (1979), *Preromanticism* (1991), *Turning Points: Essays in the History of Cultural Expressions* (1997), and, forthcoming, *The Gothic Text*. Editor of *Modern Language Quarterly: A Journal of Literary History,* and the *Cambridge History of Literary Criticism*, Vol. 5: Romanticism.

Page duBois (University of California, San Diego). Her books include *Centaurs and Amazons* (1982), *Sowing the Body* (1988), *Torture and Truth* (1991), *Sappho Is Burning* (1995), *Trojan Horses* (2001), and *Slaves and Other Objects* (2003).

Sabry Hafez (University of London). Author and editor of twenty books in Arabic on poetry, drama, literary theory, the Arabic Novel, and the short story, including works on Naguib Mahfouz, Yusuf Idris, and Mahmoud Darwish. His books in English include *The Genesis of Arabic Narrative Discourse* (1993) and the edited volumes *A Reader of Modern Arabic Short Stories* and *Modern Arabic Criticism*. He is a member of the Modern Language Panel of the Arts and Humanity Research Board, the funding council for academic research in the arts and humanities in Britain.

Ursula K. Heise (Columbia University). Author of *Chronoschisms: Time, Narrative, and Postmodernism* (1997) and of the forthcoming *World Wide Webs: Global Ecology and the Cultural Imagination*.

Djelal Kadir (Pennsylvania State University). His books include *Columbus and the Ends of the Earth* (1992), *The Other Writing: Postcolonial Essays in Latin America's Writing Culture* (1993), and *Other Modernisms in an Age of Globalizations* (2002). He served in the 1990s as editor of *World Literature Today* and is coeditor of the *Comparative History of Latin America's Literary Cultures* (2004). He is the founding president of the International American Studies Association.

David L. Pike (American University). Author of *Passage Through Hell: Modernist Descents, Medieval Underworlds* (1997) and *Subterranean Cities: Subways, Sewers,*

Cemeteries and the Culture of Paris and London (forthcoming), and of articles on topics ranging from medieval otherworlds and underground Paris, London, and New York to Canadian cinema.

Sheldon Pollock (University of Chicago). His books include *The Ramayana of Valmiki* Volume 3 (1991) and *The Language of the Gods in the World of Men* (forthcoming). He recently edited *Literary Cultures in History: Reconstructions from South Asia* (2003), and (with Homi Bhabha et al.) *Cosmopolitanism* (2002).

Bruce Robbins (Columbia University). His books include *The Servant's Hand: English Fiction from Below* (1986), *Secular Vocations* (1993), *Feeling Global: Internationalism in Distress* (1999), and a forthcoming study of upward mobility narratives in the nineteenth and twentieth centuries. Edited volumes include *Cosmopolitics: Thinking and Feeling Beyond the Nation* (1998).

Haruo Shirane (Columbia University). Author of *The Bridge of Dreams: A Poetics of "The Tale of Genji"* (1987) and of *Traces of Dreams: Landscape, Cultural Memory, and the Poetry of Bashō* (1998). He is coeditor of *Inventing the Classics: Modernity, National Identity, and Japanese Literature* (2000) and has recently edited *Early Modern Japanese Literature: An Anthology 1600–1900.*

Jane Tylus (New York University). Author of *Writing and Vulnerability in the Late Renaissance* (1993), coeditor of *Epic Traditions in the Contemporary World* (1999), and editor and translator of Lucrezia Tornabuoni de' Medici's *Sacred Narratives* (2001). Her study on late medieval female spirituality and the origins of humanism is forthcoming.

Pauline Yu (American Council of Learned Societies). President of the American Council of Learned Societies, she is the author of *The Poetry of Wang Wei* (1980) and *The Reading of Imagery in the Chinese Poetic Tradition* (1987), the editor of *Voices of the Song Lyric in China* (1994), and coeditor of *Culture and State in Chinese History* (1997) and *Ways with Words: Writing about Reading Texts from Early China* (2000).

Within the globe illustration:
Polonia · Germania · Asia · minor · Arabia · Hispania · Affrica · Oceanus Occidauus · Cuba · Spagnolla · Circumferentia Centri terræ · America · Mexicum · Regnum Peru · Brasilia · Circumferentia Centri magnitudinis · Circumferentia Centri grauitatis

Almirante de nauios para las Indias.

Don Cristobal Colon, Admiral of Ships Bound for the Indies. In Honorius Philoponus, *Nova typis trans-acta navigatio* (1621). In this image from a book by a German monk on missionary voyages, Columbus is poised at Europe's shore, the vast sea stretching away toward the Indies he can see in his mind's eye. The portrait combines eras as well as regions: Columbus is shown with a modern compass and ship, but he seems to bear the globe on his shoulder like the classical giant Atlas, while his feet rest on an ancient Christian symbol, the Anchor of Faith. While one hand gestures toward his charts, the other hand raises up toward God. The globe shows the major islands Columbus "discovered," Cuba and Hispaniola or "Spag-nolla," but much more space is given to the lands Columbus himself never believed were there: not India at all but entirely separate continents. Brazil, Peru, Mexico, and North America beckon Honorius's reader to go beyond Columbus to new explorations, conquests and conversions in the still unmapped regions approaching the "Circumference of the Center of Gravity."

The Early Modern Period

In many regions of the world, the centuries between about 1400 and 1650 mark a time of transition from ancient, largely separate traditions to the rapidly evolving and inter-connected world of modernity: the term "early modern" is increasingly used to de-scribe this transitional era. The literatures presented in this volume reflect three great global movements: of worldwide exploration and conquest; of rational and scientific inquiry; and of the growing literary use of vernacular or common speech. These three developments are closely related. The world opened out dramatically after 1492, as the Eastern and Western Hemispheres came into direct contact, and even before then, contacts were intensifying as China's Ming dynasty extended its sway across the In-dian Ocean, the expanding Ottoman Empire linked vast territories from Mesopotamia to eastern Europe, and European navigators explored the coasts of Africa and India. Greatly increased contact between widely separated cultures stimulated reflection on religious doctrines, political structures, and cultural practices of all sorts. And as old traditions came newly into question, the ancient languages that had conveyed them, like Latin and Sanskrit, began to be supplemented and even replaced by modern ver-naculars, as writers sought modes of expression that would reflect the changing real-ity around them.

EMPIRES AND NATIONS

The early modern period was marked politically by two opposing forces: expansive imperial outreach by several major powers, and national consolidation and resistance to outside rule. At times, these forces could actually work together, as when the Castilian monarchs Ferdinand and Isabella conquered the Muslim kingdom of Grenada in southern Spain in 1492; beginning in that very year, the unified nation became a major launching-point for American exploration and imperial conquest. Yet unified nations could also gain new independence from outside control: the Protestant countries of Germany and Scandinavia broke free of papal authority and the related political sway of the Holy Roman Empire, and France, though remaining largely Catholic, asserted an increasingly unified cultural identity and political independence. An important aspect of political and cultural self-definition became the establishment of national languages and literatures: French, German, English, and other national languages were increasingly used for serious literary work rather than Latin, and Italy itself was an early leader in "the vernacular revolution" as writers like Dante and Boc-caccio began to use Italian as well as Latin.

Local languages achieved new status in many parts of the world. Korea had long been in China's shadow both politically and culturally, but a new dynasty was estab-lished in 1392 by a general named Yi Song-gye. Under this dynasty, the Chosŏn—which lasted until 1910—specifically Korean arts and culture were cultivated. Like Japanese, Korean had always been written using Chinese characters, but the mid-1400s saw the establishment of a Korean alphabet. The first work written in the new

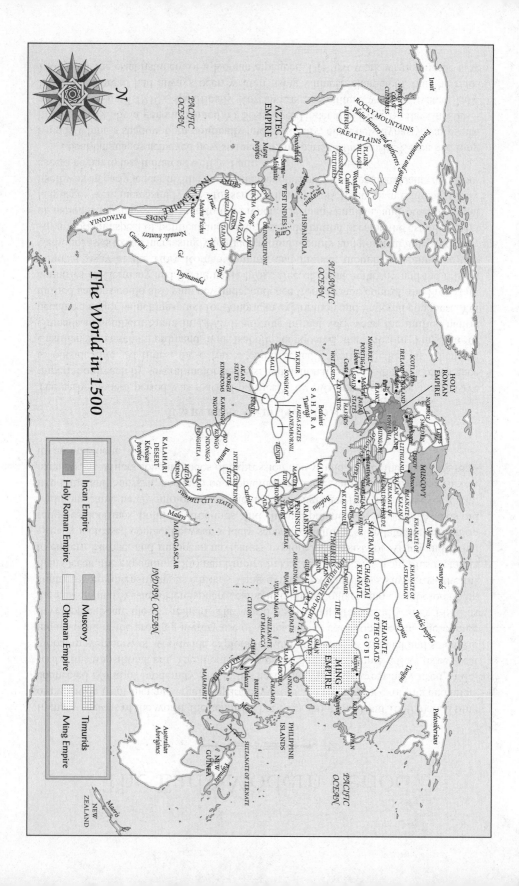

The World in 1500

Legend:
- Incan Empire
- Holy Roman Empire
- Muscovy
- Ottoman Empire
- Timurids
- Ming Empire

alphabet was a long poem called "Songs of Flying Dragons" in praise of the memory of General Yi, presenting him as a model of national unity and resistance to outside influence:

> He opened the four borders,
> Island dwellers had no more fear of pirates.
> Southern barbarians beyond our waters,
> How could they not come to him?

* * *

> If perverse theories of Western barbarians
> Threaten you with sin or allure with bliss,
> Remember, my Lord,
> His judgment and orthodoxy.

EXPLORATION AND CONQUEST

The Western barbarians were becoming increasingly visible around the world. Long-distance exploration began in earnest in the late 1400s, with Portuguese navigators exploring the coast of Africa in the 1480s and Vasco da Gama reaching as far as India in the 1490s. Columbus's epochal voyage of 1492 was followed by a flood of explorations westward and then the conquest of the Aztec and Incan empires in the early 1500s; Dutch, British, and French colonies followed Spanish settlements in North America in the early 1600s. Many regions were explored, and much literature was written about these explorations, both actual travel accounts and all sorts of poetic and fictional works derived from them, from Thomas More's philosophical fiction *Utopia* to Luis Vaz de Camões's *Lusiads* (1572) celebrating Vasco da Gama's exploits. Along with these works, this volume includes an extended section on Mesoamerica and its civilizations before, during, and after the region's conquest by a Spanish force under Hernán Cortés—a region for which we have an extraordinarily rich literary legacy of both native and European writing.

Several major empires were extending their reach in other parts of the world as well. In West Africa, the Songhai empire expanded during the 1500s from its base in Mali (see the *Epic of Son-Jara*, in Volume B). In China, the Ming dynasty, founded in 1368, ruled until 1644 at the close of the early modern period. Where previous dynasties had largely looked inward, or at most had been active in East Asia, Ming China extended its influence over an unprecedented region. The emperor Cheng Tsu (r. 1402–1424) sent a fleet of warships commanded by the enterprising eunuch admiral Cheng Ho to establish trading bases and exact tribute not only from Japan and Korea but from southern India and even the east coast of Africa. In the 1500s the Mughal Empire encompassed almost all of northern India and what is now Pakistan, while in the fifteenth through sixteenth centuries the Ottoman Empire expanded from Turkey to control Greece, the Balkans, Hungary, the Crimea, Mesopotamia, Syria, Palestine, Egypt, and the north coast of Africa all the way to Morocco at the western end of the Mediterranean. The Ottoman ruler Suleiman I, who reigned for almost half a century beginning in 1520, became known in Europe as "Suleiman the Magnificent" for the splendor of his court and his many victories.

SCIENTIFIC CONQUEST AND INQUIRY

The increasing interest in scientific inquiry and technological innovation also aided imperial outreach: modern armies and navies could now overwhelm much larger forces not equipped with rifles, cannon, and warships. The practitioners of science or "natural philosophy" could even think of themselves as conquering warriors. As the physician and alchemist Paracelsus explained in his *Great Surgery Book* in 1536, "Every experiment is like a weapon which must be used in a particular way—a spear to thrust, a club to strike. Experimenting requires a man who knows when to thrust and when to strike, each according to need and fashion." In these same years, the Polish astronomer Nicolas Copernicus was making the observations that would lead to his revolutionary assertion that the earth and other planets revolve around the sun, not the sun around the earth—a disorienting change of perspective that questioned both classical authority and Church doctrine. All phenomena and all traditions became subjects for probing, skeptical inquiry. In the 1570s Michel de Montaigne founded a new kind of writing, the essay or *essai*—French for "trial, experiment"—to convey his speculations on past and present events and on his own character. As he wrote in an inscription for his library, "I do not understand; I pause; I examine."

In Mughal India, the undogmatic ruler Akbar the Great (r. 1556–1605) organized discussions among a series of religious leaders—Zoroastrians, Christians, and Hindus, as well as Muslims. Though Akbar never abandoned Islam, the religion of his birth, he came to regard Muhammad as not necessarily the last or greatest of prophets, and he proclaimed tolerance for all religions in his realm. He reformed the judicial system in a similar spirit of inquiry, decreeing that judges "should not be satisfied with witnesses or oaths, but proceed by manifold inquiries, by the study of physiognomy, and the exercise of foresight." In Ming China, new emphasis was given to individual merit as demonstrated on civil service examinations. While established, wealthy families continued to have advantages in preparing their sons for these elaborate examinations, increasing numbers of people without marked wealth or connections were able to come into the government.

The importance given to the examinations stimulated the establishment of Chinese schools, both by the government and by private scholars; like the many new universities of Europe, these schools became centers of debate and of probing scholarship. The fifteenth and sixteenth centuries saw an outpouring of Chinese scholarship that assembled and assessed the classic works of the past. The most ambitious imperial anthology ran to no fewer than eleven thousand volumes. Textual scholars sought to establish correct texts, and one sixteenth-century scholar was so bold as to question the authenticity of portions of the classic *Book of Songs*, a text that had been a founding document for earlier Confucian orthodoxy.

The Ming scholars' interest in restoring and critically assessing their literary heritage went along with a heightened individualism and a new attention to colloquial prose fiction; Wu Cheng'en's comic novel *Journey to the West* (page 33) is even organized around a journey to India in search of accurate scriptural texts. A similar confluence can be seen in Europe as well, in the intensive reengagement with ancient texts and artworks that became known as "the Renaissance." As will be seen in many of the European works in this volume, writers and other artists engaged with new intensity with classic forms, creating modern epics, plays, poems, and fictions out of the materials of Greek and Latin tradition.

THE RISE OF PRINT CULTURE

A crucial development in the early modern period was the invention of printing, which enabled texts to be widely circulated in multiple copies and made ownership affordable to people not possessing extensive private means. The world's first movable type was developed in China by a printer named Pi Sheng in around 1000, using pottery rather than metal type, though the complexity of the thousands of Chinese characters meant that texts could still most readily be written by hand. Increasingly sophisticated methods of woodblock printing allowed for the printing of more and more texts, often to the displeasure of government officials unable to control private mass-production of texts.

In Europe, the invention of movable metal type in the 1450s revolutionized the production and circulation of texts. Among other consequences, the spread of print culture gave impetus to the protestant Reformation beginning in the early 1500s, which stressed individual reading and understanding of Scripture. Such individual reading was newly possible with the spread of printed copies of the Bible, increasingly published in vernacular languages that people could read without needing the expense and leisure required to learn Latin. Not only men but also women—rarely given classical educations—could take an active role in the writing and reading of vernacular texts, and all sorts of literary production were stimulated by the new possibilities of print and the new availability of the vernacular languages as resources for serious writing. This volume begins with examples of the developing vernacular writing in India, China, and Europe, as writers around the world began to explore the brave new worlds open to them.

The Early Modern Period

Year	The World	Literature
1300		
		1300s Aztecs begin producing painted screenfold books
1310		
1320		
	1325 Founding of Aztec capital, Tenochtitlán	**1321** Dante dies
1330		
	1337–1453 Hundred Years' War between England and France	
1340		
	1348–1350 Black Death in Europe	
1350		
		1353–1354 Petrarch writing *Canzoniere* and Boccaccio, *Decameron*
1360		
	1363 Timur (Tamerlane) begins conquests in central Asia, Persia, Russia, and India	**Early 1360s** St. Catherine, *Letters*
	1368 Chinese overthrow Mongols; Ming dynasty replaces Yuan dynasty	
1370		
	1378 Pope Gregory XI leaves Avignon for Rome; beginning of Great Schism	
1380		
1390		
1400		
		1404 Christine de Pizan, *Book of the City of Ladies*
1410		
1420		
	1428–1440 Reign of Aztec emperor Itzcoatl; Aztecs become dominant regional power	
	1429 Joan of Arc leads siege at Orleans; burned at stake (1431)	
1430		
		1430s–1519 Elaboration of court poetry in service of the Aztec empire
	1434 Cosimo de'Medici becomes ruler of Florence	**1430s** Leon Battista Alberti, *On Painting*
1440		
	1440 Portuguese begin slave trade in Africa	
	1444 Mehmed II becomes sultan of Ottoman Empire	
1450		
	1450 Lorenzo Valla proves *Donation of Constantine* a forgery	**1450s** François Villon, poetic works
	1453 Gutenberg prints first Bible using movable metal type; Turks seize Constantinople; end of Byzantine Empire	

Plate 1 Albrecht Dürer, *Self-Portrait,* 1500. The art historian H. R. Janson called Dürer "the first artist to be fascinated by his own image." Whether or not this is the case, it is certainly striking to see the young German, here 29 years old, confronting us in Christlike solemnity, and to consider that the initials "AD" on the left side of the portrait not only mean *anno domini* (year of our Lord), but also signify Dürer's own initials. One of the first modern artists to benefit from the revolution in printing—Dürer launched his career as a woodcut designer in Basel and Strasbourg, urban centers with numerous publishing houses— he was largely responsible for bringing the influences of Italian Renaissance art to bear on the north. At the same time, as in this self-portrait, Dürer remained receptive to social and cultural developments in his own country, and he would enthusiastically embrace Martin Luther; one of his last major works, *The Four Apostles* from 1526, is a strong defense of the young Reformation and its most ardent spokesperson. *(Alte Pinakothek, Munich, Germany / SuperStock.)*

Plate 2 Agnolo Bronzino, *Allegory (Venus, Cupid, Folly and Time)*, c. 1545. Bronzino was for many years court painter to the Medici, producing stately portraits of Duke Cosimo and his Spanish wife, Eleonora. But Cosimo's taste did not run only to ducal settings, and in the mid-1540s he commissioned the painting variously known as "Allegory," "Exposure of Luxury," or most straightforwardly, "Venus, Cupid, Folly, and Time." The work foregrounds a shocking spectacle of incest. The young god of love fondles his mother's breast while she holds one of his poisonous arrows above her head and clutches the golden apple that created the discord leading to the Trojan War. Behind these two and a naked putto playfully tossing rose petals is a more sobering scene: an anguished Michelangelesque figure clutching her hair, elderly Time pulling back the curtain to "expose" the couple, and the chilling image of a girl whose body ends in a serpent's tail and whose supposedly benign offering to the spectator of a honeycomb can only be construed as suspicious. Painted on the eve of the Catholic Reformation and a period of increasing concern about sensuality and the influence of pagan art, Bronzino's work teases us with its explicit celebration of classically derived themes and with its brooding condemnation of its highly stylized perverseness. *(National Gallery, London / Bridgeman Art Library.)*

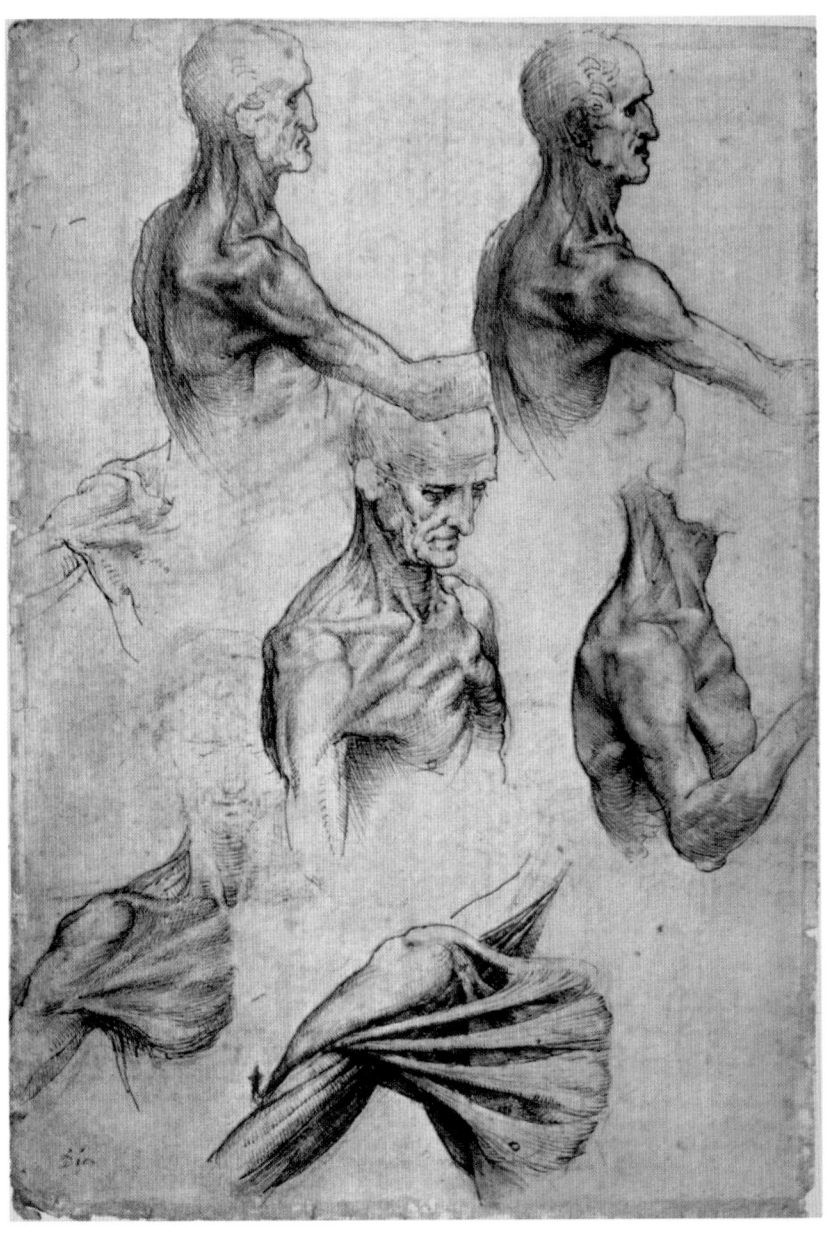

Plate 3 Leonardo da Vinci, *Muscles of the Neck and Shoulders,* early 1500s. A very different art of the body than Bronzino's *Allegory* can be seen in these anatomical sketches. Nothing escaped the attention of Leonardo da Vinci, who was as accomplished in anatomy and the science of warfare as he was in art. His indefatiguable curiosity has rightly earned him the title of the consummate Renaissance man, even as it spawned a restlessness that rarely allowed him to finish the massive projects he took up in the courts of Rome, Milan, and Paris. His scrawlings in notebooks allowed him both to indulge his creative powers and to cultivate independence from the demands of patrons, and over his long life he produced literally thousands of drawings. It is to da Vinci that we owe some of the finest botanical studies ever done, as well as designs for early flying machines (which when tested, actually flew). But perhaps his greatest achievement as an artist are his studies of the human body. His fascination with isolating tendons, bones, ligaments, and muscles allowed him to reveal the similarities between body and machine, tracing the organic in the inorganic. Yet as his *Mona Lisa* and many portraits of the Madonna attest, he was also gifted in depicting a female beauty at once aloof from its surroundings and immediate in its graceful physical presence. *(The Royal Library, Windsor Castle / SuperStock.)*

Plate 4 Sophonisba Anguissola, *The Chess Game,* 1555. Anguissola was the most prominent woman artist of the Italian Renaissance, painting in Cremona, Madrid, Genoa, and Palermo—where she was visited in her nineties by the Flemish painter Van Dyck. Like her five sisters, she was the beneficiary of an unusually sophisticated humanist education, and like them, she trained with artists in her native Cremona. Particularly skilled at portraits (and self-portraits; one of her more reflexive works paints the artist Bernardino Campi painting her), she made notable studies of King Phillip II of Spain and his wife Isabella. She was admired by both Michelangelo and his close friend Tommaso Cavalieri, who believed that she defied the general rule that women were inferior to men in artistic achievement. Her *Chess Game* features three of her sisters as well as a servant. The elaborate dress is exemplary of the nobility's garments of the time, but the subject matter is an uncommon one, as it turns the highly intellectual work of chess into a women's game, played not in the safe and intimate surroundings of domestic space but outdoors, with a view of what is probably Cremona below. *(Erich Lessing / Art Resource, New York.)*

Plate 5   Pieter Brueghel the Elder, *Landscape with the Fall of Icarus,* 1550s. W. H. Auden memorialized Brueghel's painting in his poem "Musée des Beaux Arts," where he contrasts the serene Flemish landscape and the odd, almost irrelevant detail of a boy's pale body plummeting into the water, having fallen from a place too near the sun: "Everything turns away / Quite leisurely from the disaster," such as the boat that "had somewhere to get to and sailed calmly on." Whether Brueghel too was concerned with man's casual indifference to man is another question. He and his sons dominated Antwerp's art scene in the mid-16th and 17th centuries, excelling in landscape painting and still life. Some of his most memorable works focus on peasant life and customs, while he also painted religious subjects such as the *Tower of Babel* and *The Parable of the Sower,* always with an eye to penetrating realistic detail in the manner of other northern European artists. Brueghel did not flinch from using his works as social commentaries, as attested by some of his satirical paintings on the troubled relationship between the Netherlands and Spain. The early *Fall of Icarus,* which exists in two versions, may well have been meant to convey the message of man's inhumanity. But just as easily it suggests the tragic necessity of death amidst life's overwhelming richness, or the final insignificance of those who, like Icarus, have foolishly ignored the warnings of their elders and flown too high. *(Musées Royaux des Beaux-Arts de Belgique, Brussels, Belgium / Giraudon-Bridgeman Art Library.)*

Plate 6 Frontispiece to the *Codex Fejérváry-Mayer,* Mexico, before 1521. This image painted by the Aztecs' Mixtec allies divides the world into its five sections: east (at the top), south, west, north, and center. The center represents the temple complex at the heart of the Aztec capital, Tenochtitlán, dominated by the sun and war god Huitzilopochtli. Radiating out from the center are the four quarters of the world, each with its own patron god, bird, tree, and color. The image maps time as well as space: it is the frontispiece to a divination book called a *tonalamatl,* "a book of days and destinies" used to chart people's lives and fortunes. Rows of hieroglyphs in each quadrant give two forms of day-count, one using a yearly cycle of 365 days, the other using a ritual calendar of 260 days. Each of the world's five divisions was associated with an age of the world; the Aztecs and their neighbors believed that they lived in the Fifth Age, named "4-Movement." *(Liverpool City Museum, Liverpool / Werner Forman / Art Resource, New York.)*

Plate 7 Malinche and Devil masks, Guerrero, Mexico, mid-20th century. Masks were an important part of ritual dances in pre-Conquest Mexico, helping the dancers identify with divinities and guardian animals, and they are still widely used in festivals now associated with Catholic feast days. The two masks shown here attest to the ongoing vitality of old traditions, now mixed with new elements—in these cases, with deliberate irony. The top mask shows Malinche, Cortés's Indian wife and interpreter, her pink skin symbolizing the passion that led her to aid Cortés against her own people. Usually Malinche masks have a native appearance, but this Malinche's blue eyes and slender features give a modern twist to the old theme of cultural betrayal. She takes on the imported beauty of a Hollywood starlet, uncannily offset by the horns protruding from her head, decorated with ribbons recalling the ancient colors of the four sacred directions. The second mask has a face inside an eagle helmet, formerly the mark of an Aztec warrior; but here, in place of a warrior, a devil leers out from his helmet. *(Private collection / photograph by David Damrosch.)*

Plate 8 Miguel Gabrera, Portrait of *Sor Juana Inés de la Cruz,* 1750. Painted half a century after Sor Juana's death from the plague, this portrait gives us the austere Mexican nun garbed in the signs of her profession: her black habit, her rosary beads, an enormous brooch depicting a prayerful female figure. But the books on the shelves behind her suggest Sor Juana's double life. We find not only a history of the papacy, but also the medical treatises of Galen and Hippocrates and Livy's *History of Rome,* among other classical and modern texts on thoroughly secular subjects. In her autobiographical account, *La respuesta,* Sor Juana wrote that in entering the convent, "I thought I was fleeing myself but—woe is me!—I brought myself with me, and brought my greatest enemy in my inclination to study, which I know not whether to take as a Heaven-sent favor or as a punishment." The serenity and self-command Gabrera here depicts seem to argue decisively for the former interpretation. *(The Art Archive / National History Museum, Mexico City / Dagli Orti.)*

YEAR	THE WORLD	LITERATURE
1460		
1470	1474 Isabella becomes Queen of Castile 1478 Spanish Inquisition begins	1470s Lucrezia Tornabuoni de'Medici, *Sacred Stories*
1480	1488 Bartolomeu Dias explores Cape of Good Hope	
1490	1492 Jews expelled from Spain; Columbus explores West Indies	1493 Columbus writes first letters to Queen Isabella detailing his discoveries 1494 Aldus Manutius establishes an important printing press in Venice
	1497 Leonardo da Vinci, *Last Supper* 1498 Vasco da Gama reaches India; Savonarola burned at stake in Florence 1499–1501 Amerigo Vespucci explores coast of Brazil	
1500	1500 Michelangelo, *David* 1502–1520 Reign of Moctezuma II in Mexico	1509 Erasmus, *The Praise of Folly*
1510	1511 Cuba becomes Spanish colony 1514 Copernicus publishes work on heliocentric theory 1517 Luther writes 95 theses contesting Church's practice of granting indulgences 1519–1522 Magellan circumnavigates globe 1519 Hernán Cortés invades Aztec empire, places Moctezuma under house arrest	1513 Niccolò Machiavelli, *The Prince* 1516 Thomas More, *Utopia* 1519–1521 Cortés writes five long letters to Charles V on his exploits
1520	1521 Three–month siege of Tenochtitlán ends in fall of Aztec empire. Cortés gains control over central and southern Mexico 1523 Pedro de Alvarado conquers Guatemala. Pope Clement VII sends a dozen missionaries to organize the conversion of the Mexican population 1525–1526 Peasants' rebellion in Germany; Thomas Muntzer executed 1527 Sack of Rome by Holy Roman Emperor Charles V 1529 Turks invade Austria; Bernardino de Sahagún arrives in Mexico	1522 Martin Luther translates New Testament 1524 Aztec-Spanish dialogues on the merits of traditional religion versus Christianity 1524–1525 Erasmus and Luther debate free will 1527 Baldassare Castiglione, *The Courtier*
1530	1532 Francisco Pizarro conquers Incan empire in Peru 1533 Jean Calvin goes to Geneva 1534 Henry VIII excommunicated 1535 Thomas More beheaded 1539 First printing press in New World (Mexico)	1530s Lyrics of Michelangelo and Vittoria Colonna 1532 François Rabelais, *Pantagruel* 1534 Rabelais, *Gargantua*
1540	1540 Jesuits approved by Pope as official order; Treatise signed between Turkey and Venice	1540s Clement Marot translates the Psalms; Marguerite de Navarre, *Heptameron* 1540–1560s Wu Cheng'en, *Journey to the West*

YEAR	THE WORLD	LITERATURE
	1545–1562 Council of Trent reforms Catholic practices in response to Protestant challenges	**1547–1580s** Bernardino de Sahagún collects materials from native informants for his *General History of the Affairs of New Spain* and poetry collections
1550		
	1555 Calvinist mission to Brazil	**1555** Louise Labé, *Works*
	1557 Erasmus's works put on Index of Prohibited Books	
	1559 Elizabeth I becomes Queen of England	
1560		
	1562–1598 French Wars of Religion	**1560s** Bartolomé de las Casas, *Apolgetic History*
	1568–1648 War in Netherlands, ending with independence from Spain	**1564–1565** Bernal Díaz del Castillo, *True History of the Conquest of New Spain*
1570		
	1572 Battle of Lepanto, Spanish Catholic naval forces defeat Ottomans; St. Bartholomew's Day massacre	**1570s** Luis Vaz de Camões, *The Lusiads;* Jean de Léry, *History of a Voyage to Brazil*
	1578 King Sebastiaõ and Portuguese troops killed in northern Africa	**1577** Teresa of Avila, *Interior Castle*
1580		
	1582 Gregorian Calendar implemented	**1580s** Jan Kochanowski, *Laments;* Michel de Montaigne, *Essays*
	1580 Union of Portugal and Spain	
	1585 First English settlement in North America	
1590	**1588** Spanish Armada defeated by England	
	1598 Restoration of shogunate in Japan	
1600		
	1609 Spain approaching bankruptcy; Moors expelled	
1610		
		1611 William Shakespeare, *The Tempest*
		1612 Miguel de Cervantes, *Don Quixote,* Part 1
		1614 Lope de Vega, *Fuenteovejuna*
	1618–1648 Thirty Years' War	**1616** Cervantes, *Don Quixote,* Part 2
1620		
	1620 Plymouth Colony founded in Massachusetts	
	1621 Philip IV becomes King of Spain	**1624** John Donne, *Devotions upon Emergent Occasions*
	1628 Recurrence of plague in Europe	**1629** Hernando Ruiz de Alarcón, *Treatise on the Superstitions of the Natives of This New Spain*
1630		
1640	**1633** Galileo recants before the Inquisition	
	1640 Portuguese war of independence begins	**1641** René Descartes, *Meditations*
	1642–1649 English Civil War	
1650	**1649** Charles I beheaded	
		1650 Anne Bradstreet, *The Tenth Muse Lately Sprung Up in America*
1660		
	1660 Restoration and return of Charles II to England	**1667** John Milton, *Paradise Lost*
		1667–1670 Sor Juana Inés de la Cruz writes first purely Mexican poems in Spanish

⬡ CROSSCURRENTS ⬡
The Vernacular Revolution

For a thousand years or more, from late antiquity until around 1200 C.E., almost all the world's literature was composed in elite languages, employing literary modes far removed from the speech of common people. Literacy was confined to a small number of people—almost always men—in court and temple circles, and writers usually strove to preserve and elaborate older literary traditions rather than to adapt their work to the changes of everyday language. Sanskrit in India, classical Chinese in Japan and in China itself, and Latin in Europe were for a millennium the dominant literary languages in their regions, even as people spoke ever more widely divergent dialects and languages in daily life.

This situation began to change between around 1000 and 1300 in many parts of the world. These changes took different forms in different cultures and occurred on varying timetables, yet collectively it is appropriate to speak of a worldwide "vernacular revolution" during these years and the centuries that followed. The works in this section show the varied purposes that common or vernacular language came to serve in several different cultures. In some cases, the older, elite literary language was still used as well, sometimes for privileged genres: thus in Japan, Chinese was often still used for poetry, even after prose writers like Murasaki Shikibu pioneered the use of Japanese for writing their prose romances. In China itself, the literary language and techniques perfected by the Tang dynasty poets of the seventh through ninth centuries continued to dominate upper-class poetry for another thousand years, but by the 1500s prose writers were coming to favor a "vernacular" style much closer to everyday speech. This shift in style went along with a shift in emphasis as well, toward more realistic portrayals in prose fiction of life in society, often with more attention to lower classes—"vernacular" itself comes from a Latin word, *verna*, meaning a household slave, and by extension "home-grown" or "native."

In India, Sanskrit began to give way to writing in many of the different languages spoken around the Indian subcontinent, such as Tamil and Telugu. Writers in these vernacular languages often came from artisan or merchant classes, and at times openly rejected the caste hierarchy that had put the Brahmins, and the Sanskrit language, above them. Sometimes these vernacular writings were secular in emphasis, with religious writing still favoring Sanskrit, but over time an increasing amount of religious and devotional writing came to be composed in the vernacular as well.

In Europe, German and Icelandic writers on the margins of the Latin tradition began to write in their local Germanic languages, and Anglo-Saxon, Irish, and Welsh literatures all flourished in the British Isles. By 1300, even in the strongholds of the Latin tradition, Dante in Italy and Provençal poets in France were using the vernacular to write great poetry. In a letter to his patron Can Grande della Scala, Dante defended writing his *Commedia* in Italian rather than Latin, saying that he wanted to reach as many of his countrymen—and women—as possible. The trade-off was that vernacular work would be less read abroad, and Dante and many others continued to use Latin when they wanted to reach an international audience directly. The great sixteenth-century scholar Erasmus of Rotterdam wrote and lectured in Latin all his life, communicating in this way with scholars across Europe as he worked in Holland, England, France, Italy, Belgium, Germany, and Switzerland.

As vernacular writing spread, translation began to play a prominent role in the circulation of literary texts, and Erasmus himself strongly promoted the translation of the Bible into vernacular languages. The Church had long favored the exclusive use of Latin for theological writing and for the Bible, so that all Christians could understand it in common and also so that Church authorities could control the text's form and the doctrines they derived from it. With the rise of Protestantism, however, reformers like Luther and Erasmus began to emphasize the individual's direct encounter with Scripture, and they sought to make the Bible accessible to all Christians, whatever their social class and whatever their language. As Erasmus declared—in Latin—in a preface to an edition of the Greek New Testament:

> Perhaps the state secrets of kings have to be concealed, but Christ wanted his mysteries to be disseminated as widely as possible. I should prefer that all women, even of the lowest rank, should read the evangelists and the epistles of Paul, and I wish these writings were translated into all the languages of the human race, so that they could be read and studied, not just by the Irish and the Scots, but by the Turks as well, and the Saracens. . . . I would hope that the farmer might chant a holy text at his plow, the spinner sing it as she sits at her wheel, the traveler ease the tedium of his journey with tales from Scripture.

In this passage, Erasmus allows that Latin, long the language of European diplomacy, may still have value for keeping "state secrets" out of general circulation; but the spread of the vernacular tended as well to lessen the control over information formerly held closely by royal courts. The rise of the different vernaculars also stimulated the consolidation of nation-states around a dominant language or dialect, and gave the means for a growing number of people in those states to express themselves and to seek direct participation in public life. Even as it opened up a greatly expanded and varied literary landscape, the vernacular revolution ultimately paved the way for the middle-class and then working-class revolutions that have shaped our modern world.

❖

Vernacular Writing in South Asia

For nearly a thousand years beginning in the last centuries B.C.E., the entire literary landscape of South Asia was occupied by Sanskrit (and to a far less extent, by the two languages related to Sanskrit—Prakrit and Apabhramsha—that had been used especially for literature meant to suggest the world of rural life in contrast to the court). We have no evidence that the regional languages of South Asia, with the important exception of Tamil, were ever used for the creation of written expressive texts during this period. But this situation changed dramatically near the end of the first millennium C.E., when writers in southern India first began to experiment with courtly registers of local dialects. Over the course of the next 500 years, local-language writing began to appear everywhere in South Asia. Scholars don't fully understand the conditions that made this vernacular revolution possible, and the fact that a remarkably similar transformation occurred in western Europe around the same period complicates explanation even more. But a revolution did occur, and it powerfully challenged the dominance of Sanskrit, and indeed other dimensions of Sanskrit culture and society as well.

In most regions of South Asia, the earliest vernacular writers were court poets who imitated Sanskrit literature in idiom, metrics, and themes. The religious dimension of their work, where present at all, was typically muted. However, this inaugural vernacular movement was followed by a second wave prominently marked by religious sentiment, especially by the idea of direct access to the divine sometimes termed *bhakti* (devotion). Unlike the vernacular transformation in Europe, which was hastened by translations of the Bible into regional languages (page 115), no attempt was ever made in South Asia before the modern period to translate Sanskrit scriptures. Instead, altogether new bodies of religious writing were created, some that would eventually attain canonical scriptural status. The devotional poets, often low-caste artisans or ascetics, rejected the high style of Sanskrit and the social values of caste hierarchy imputed (sometimes unjustly) to Sanskrit culture as a whole. In south India, the *Virashaivas*—Militant Devotees of the god Shiva—invented what they called the *vacana* (plain talking), an unversified, unadorned, and for the most part, it seems, unwritten form. In fact, this seems to have been meant as a kind of anti-literature, as radically anomalous in its aesthetic as was the Virashaivas' social critique, especially their rejection of the caste system and their denunciation of the wealthy and the grand temples that were the concrete manifestation of their power (and which low-caste people were prohibited from entering). Both men and women composed in the *vacana* form; among the latter, Mahadeviyakka produced *vacana*s that represent some of the earliest and most powerful expressions of erotic devotionalism in South Asia, and bear close comparison to the poems of Mahadevi's European contemporaries, Hildegard von Bingen and Mechthild von Magdeburg (see Volume B). Somewhat later in northern India, the weaver-poet Kabir (1400–1450) composed verses in Old Hindi whose idiom and style were as innovative as the criticism he expressed through them of Hindu and Muslim exclusivity. Like those of many of the vernacular devotional poets, the compositions of Kabir remain alive to this day on the lips of people across northern India.

Tukaram, who lived in western India in the early seventeenth century and wrote in the Marathi language, gave voice to the literary aspirations of many of these poets when he exclaimed, in one of his many confessional poems:

> I have no
> Personal skill.
> It is
> The Cosmic One
> Making me speak.

Yet the artistry and aesthetic long associated with Sanskrit did maintain themselves in many vernacular literary cultures. Especially instructive is the case of Telugu, the language of today's Andhra Pradesh in southeastern India. Court poets continued for centuries to write marvelously sophisticated literature in Telugu in the high style even as poets associated with one or another of the great temples in the region sought a simpler, more common idiom. But the division between the court and temple traditions is not always hard and fast; moreover, creative innovation continued in both spheres, in content as well as form. The songs (called *padam*) of the mid-seventeenth-century poet Kshetrayya illustrate these trends particularly well. Like many devotional poets before him, Kshetrayya adopts a female voice, of various kinds: that of the confused love-sick ingénue ("Those women, they deceived me"), for example, or the jilted mistress ("'Your body is my body'"), but most often the courtesan ("Pour gold as high as I stand"). He uses these different voices to evoke powerful, complex emotions of spiritual longing for the divine (called here Muvva Gopala, the name of Kshetrayya's village god), and all the feelings accompanying that longing: from despair at God's apparent indifference, to a readiness to negotiate with Him (as if he were a prostitute's customer), to the self-negating ecstasy of union. Although the language and form of these songs are simple and entirely local, the categories of eroticism and much of the imagery borrow creatively from the high tradition (as seen, for example, in "Love in a Courtly Language," Volume A). The wit and wisdom and passion, however, are Kshetrayya's alone, as is the transformation of the very subject matter itself. Sometimes it seems impossible to decide whether the vision of sex, with God as customer, is an expression of the ecstasy of religious union in the manner of the older mystical traditions mentioned above, or whether—in the new early-modern economy of southern India that was fluid, commercial, and dynamic and where old traditions were crumbling—the customer himself is viewed as God, and sex is nothing more, or less, than sex.

PRONUNCIATIONS:
bhakti: BHUK-tee
Virashaiva: VEER-uh-SHAI-vuh

✦ ⪥✧⪤ ✦

Basavanna[1]

Like a monkey on a tree

Like a monkey on a tree
it leaps from branch to branch:
    how can I believe or trust
    this burning thing, this heart?
5   It will not let me go
    to my Father,
    my lord of the meeting rivers.[1]

You can make them talk

You can make them talk
if the serpent
has stung
them.

5   You can make them talk
if they're struck
by an evil planet.[1]

But you can't make them talk
if they're struck dumb
10   by riches.

    Yet when Poverty the magician
    enters, they'll speak
    at once,

    O lord of the meeting rivers.

The crookedness of the serpent

The crookedness of the serpent
is straight enough for the snake-hole.

The crookedness of the river
is straight enough for the sea.

5   And the crookedness of our Lord's men
is straight enough for our Lord!

Before the grey reaches the cheek

Before
    the grey reaches the cheek,

---

1. Translated by A. K. Ramanujan. Basavanna (traditionally dated 1106–c. 1167) was a minister and treasurer of King Bijjala at Kalyana in Karnataka, against whom he is said to have led a coup. He is credited with founding the Virashaiva religious community.

1. After appearing in Basavanna's dreams, Shiva manifested himself at a temple in the village of Kudalasangama ("the river confluence at Kudala") and initiated him as the leader of the Virashaivas.

1. Some planets, such as Saturn, were believed to exert harmful influences.

the wrinkle the rounded chin
and the body becomes a cage of bones:

5   before
        with fallen teeth
        and bent back
        you are someone else's ward:

        before
10   you drop your hand to the knee
        and clutch a staff:

        before
        age corrodes
        your form:

15   before
        death touches you:

                worship
                our lord
                of the meeting rivers!

I don't know anything like time-beats and meter

I don't know anything like time-beats and meter
nor the arithmetic of strings and drums;
I don't know the count of iamb and dactyl.[1]

My lord of the meeting rivers,
5   as nothing will hurt you
        I'll sing as I love.

The rich will make temples for Śiva

The rich
will make temples for Śiva.
What shall I,
a poor man,
5   do?

My legs are pillars,
the body the shrine,
the head a cupola
of gold.

10   Listen, O lord of the meeting rivers,
        things standing shall fall,
        but the moving ever shall stay.[1]

---

1. Iamb and dactyl are here used as loose English equivalents for Kannada *amritagana* and *devagana,* kinds of metrical unit [translator's note].
1. Virashaiva thought stresses the opposition between that which "stands" and that which "moves." What moves is

synonymous with the dynamism of the wandering mendicant of the Virashaiva community, who has renounced the home and the world in devotion to Shiva. What stands still is representative of the rigid strictures of orthodox Hinduism and its temples.

∽∾

RESONANCE

Palkuriki Somanatha: from *The Legend of Basavanna*[1]

One day, when these and the rest of the host of devotees were enjoying the pleasures of the empire of devotion, and flourishing with ancient glory, I fell prostrate like a stick before the glorious, innumerable *māheśvaras.*[2] I was anointed by the nectar of their compassionate devotion. And I submitted to the assembly, saying, "I want to narrate the incomparable *Basava Purāṇa.* Kindly tell me how to handle the thread of that story and make me fulfilled."

When I had submitted myself thus, praising them and desiring their help, the gathering of devotees was pleased. They looked at me affectionately, cast their kindly glances upon me, and said, "We have given you the ability to spread the *Basava Purāṇa.* Now you must compose it so that it pleases the steadfast devotees."

When they spoke, I accepted the command of the assembled devotees with great reverence. Therefore, I will now begin to compose this poem. * * *

In the sacred purāṇas, it is said that "Uma is our mother and Rudra is our father"; therefore, I am born of the Īśvara family.[3] I was born out of the womb-hand of the liṅga guru.[4] He is an embodiment of the *śaraṇas, the gaṇas,* and all the other attendants of Śiva.[5] The devotees have anointed me with their compassion. I am free of worldly bonds. I belong to the devotee *gotra.*[6] The brilliant Viṣṇurāmideva and the illustrious Śriyādevi love me as their son. I am dedicated to the heroic *māheśvara* tradition.[7] I am a honeybee on the lotus feet of Kaṭṭakūri Potidevara, the renowned devotee. I gained the power to compose poetry from Karasthali Viśvanātha, the compassionate devotee. I am a bosom friend of Cĕnna Rāma, the eminent student of Vadagāmu Rāmeśa. I avoid showing respect, holding conversation, or any other kind of association with *bhavis.*[8] My name is Pālkuriki Somanātha. I am a man of pure character.

Since beautiful, idiomatic Telugu is more commonly understood than heavy compositions of mixed prose and verse, I have chosen to compose this entirely in the *dvipada* meter. Let it not be said that these words are nothing but Telugu. Rather, look at them as equal to the Vedas. If you wonder how that can be, remember, if a *tūmu* is a standard of measure, so is *sola.* Is it not generally agreed that the stature of a poet derives from his ability to create great poetry from simple words?

The underlying strength of this work is my fixation on Basava. The collection of songs that are sung about the ancient devotees are in accordance with the Vedas and purāṇas. The songs are also acceptable to the esoteric theory of the liṅga. They will be

1. Translated by Velcheru Narayana Rao. Few works present so intense, and so eccentric and violent, an account of religious devotion as Somanatha's biography of Basavanna and the early leaders of the Militant Shaiva community. Written in the 13th century perhaps only a few generations after the death of Basava, Somanatha's work reveals in all its intensity the rage of the lower castes against the social and spiritual power of Brahmanism.
2. Devotees of Shiva.
3. *Puranas* are books of holy legend; Uma is the wife of Rudra, another name of Shiva; the Ishvara family signi-

fies the family of Shiva.
4. A reference to a child's initiation into the Shaiva order on the part of the teacher. The *linga* is an abstract representation of Shiva.
5. The *sharanas* ("refuges") and the *ganas* ("troops") represent different types of Shiva devotees.
6. A *gotra* is a lineage; to claim a "devotee *gotra*" is to reject one's natural family in favor of the new family of devotees of Shiva.
7. The tradition of the Virashaiva community.
8. Anyone not belonging to the Virashaiva community.